U.S. HISTORY Need to Know

SilverTip

The Lewis and Clark Expedition

by Daniel R. Faust

Consultant: Caitlin Krieck
Social Studies Teacher and Instructional Coach
The Lab School of Washington

BEARPORT
PUBLISHING

Minneapolis, Minnesota

Credits
Cover and title page, © Edgar Samuel Paxson/Wikimedia Creative Commons license 3.0; 5, © one photo/Shutterstock; 7, © ilbuscaGetty Images ; 8, © John Parrot/Stocktrek Images/Getty Images; 9, © Ronnie Chua/Shutterstock; 11, © Anna in Sweden/Shutterstock; 13 Background, © Virginia Museum of History & Culture/Alamy; 13T, © Everett Collection/Shutterstock; 13B, © Everett Collection/Shutterstock; 15, © Charles Marion Russell/Wikimedia Creative Commons license 3.0; 17, © Edgar Samuel Paxson/Wikimedia Creative Commons license 3.0; 19, © eastandwest/Shutterstock; 21, © planet5D LLC/Shutterstock; 23T, © Virginia Museum of History & Culture/Alamy; 23B, © William Clark and Meriwether Lewis/Library of Congress; 25, © Captures by Kate/Shutterstock; 27, © Patti McConville/Alamy; and 28, © ActiveLines/Shutterstock.

Bearport Publishing Company Product Development Team
President: Jen Jenson; Director of Product Development: Spencer Brinker; Managing Editor: Allison Juda; Associate Editor: Naomi Reich; Associate Editor: Tiana Tran; Senior Designer: Colin O'Dea; Associate Designer: Elena Klinkner; Associate Designer: Kayla Eggert; Product Development Specialist: Anita Stasson

A NOTE FROM THE PUBLISHER: Some of the historic photos in this book have been colorized to help readers have a more meaningful and rich experience. The color results are not intended to depict actual historical detail.

Library of Congress Cataloging-in-Publication Data

Names: Faust, Daniel R., author.
Title: The Lewis and Clark Expedition / by Daniel R. Faust.
Description: Minneapolis, MN : Bearport Publishing Company, [2024] | Series: U.S. history: need to know | "Silvertip books." | Includes bibliographical references and index.
Identifiers: LCCN 2023005425 (print) | LCCN 2023005426 (ebook) | ISBN 9798888220283 (library binding) | ISBN 9798888222195 (paperback) | ISBN 9798888223437 (ebook)
Subjects: LCSH: Lewis and Clark Expedition (1804-1806)–Juvenile literature. | West (U.S.)–Discovery and exploration–Juvenile literature.
Classification: LCC F592.7 .F385 2024 (print) | LCC F592.7 (ebook) | DDC 917.804/2–dc23
LC record available at https://lccn.loc.gov/2023005425
LC ebook record available at https://lccn.loc.gov/2023005426

Copyright © 2024 Bearport Publishing Company. All rights reserved. No part of this publication may be reproduced in whole or in part, stored in any retrieval system, or transmitted in any form or by any means, electronic, mechanical, photocopying, recording, or otherwise, without written permission from the publisher.

For more information, write to Bearport Publishing, 5357 Penn Avenue South, Minneapolis, MN 55419.

Contents

There's a Map for That 4

A New Nation. 6

Go West! 8

The Corps of Discovery 12

The Journey Begins 16

Reaching the Pacific. 18

Home Again. 20

Mission Accomplished 22

Just the Beginning 26

A Journey of Discovery 28

SilverTips for Success 29

Glossary 30

Read More 31

Learn More Online 31

Index .32

About the Author. 32

There's a Map for That

How do you know how to get where you're going? Today, you can find a map with just a few taps on your phone. But it wasn't always so easy. Someone had to make the maps first. How did we get the first maps of the United States?

Modern maps are made using technology. Airplanes and satellites can gather information from the sky. In the past, the only way to make maps was to explore unknown places by land.

A New Nation

In 1803, the United States was still a new country. The Mississippi River marked its western **border**. Then, the United States paid France for a large **territory** it controlled at the time. This came to be known as the Louisiana Purchase. It made the United States double in size.

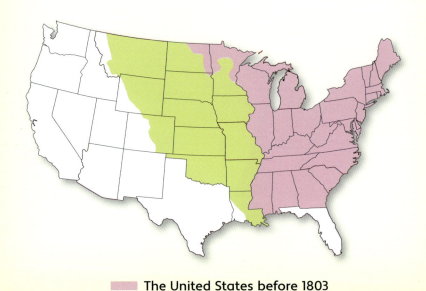

The United States before 1803
Louisiana Purchase territory

Before Europeans arrived, there were many people in North America. The new **settlers** wanted to move where Native American groups already lived. There was often fighting over the land.

Go West!

With the Louisiana Purchase, the United States gained a lot of new territory. However, few European settlers had ever been west of the Mississippi River. They did not know what to expect. President Thomas Jefferson wanted to find out more about this land. He hoped Americans would move there.

President Jefferson hoped to find a river that connected the eastern and western parts of North America. At the time, rivers were the fastest way to move people and things.

President Jefferson decided to send an **expedition** into the Louisiana Territory. He wanted the explorers to discover the land's plants and animals. As they went, they would make maps of the area. Jefferson also wanted them to set up good trade relationships with the Native Americans living there.

The fur trade was a big business at the time. People hunted animals to make things from their fur. President Jefferson hoped the new territory would be home to many animals.

Beaver fur was very popular.

The Corps of Discovery

The **mission** west came to be known as the Lewis and Clark Expedition. It was named after the two men in charge. Meriwether Lewis and William Clark would lead a team of men into the new territory. This group was called the Corps (kor) of Discovery.

Before the trip, Lewis was President Jefferson's **secretary**. His job would be to gather the team's supplies. Clark was an officer in the United States Army. He hired and trained the group's members.

Lewis and Clark's team was made up of just under 50 men. It had soldiers, hunters, and **blacksmiths**. The group packed their supplies into three boats near what is now St. Louis, Missouri. They started by heading west along the Missouri River.

> The Corps of Discovery packed many things for the trip. They brought guns, food, and warm clothing. They also had things to trade with the Native American groups they would meet.

The Journey Begins

The expedition left on May 14, 1804. In August of that year, they met the Oto and Missouri Native American people in what is now Iowa. Then, the corps spent the winter with the Mandan and Hidatsa people in North Dakota. There, they met a young woman named Sacagawea (sah-KAH-gah-wee-ah). She went with them as they continued their expedition.

> Sacagawea and many other Native peoples helped the Corps of Discovery. Sacagawea communicated with Native American peoples they met along the way, using sign language and trade languages.

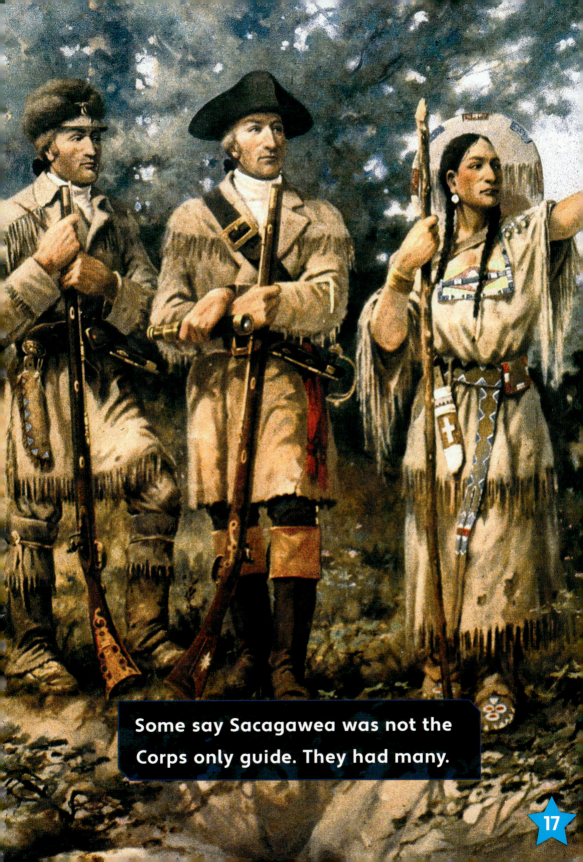

Some say Sacagawea was not the Corps only guide. They had many.

Reaching the Pacific

The explorers reached the end of the Missouri River in the early summer of 1805. From there, the Shoshone people helped them cross the Rocky Mountains. The Nez Perce took them from there. Finally, the expedition reached the Columbia River. They traveled along that river to the Pacific Ocean.

> The Corps of Discovery reached the Pacific in November 1805. They spent the winter near what is now Astoria, Oregon. They had traveled more than 4,100 miles (6,600 km)!

Home Again

When spring came, the expedition headed home. The return trip began in March 1806. The Corps of Discovery ended their trip on September 23 of the same year. It had taken them over a year to get to the Pacific. Because they already knew the way, coming back took only six months.

> On the return trip, Lewis and Clark split up. They each took a group of men. One crew went north, and the other went south. The Corps met up in what is now North Dakota.

The Gateway Arch in St. Louis was built to honor the city's role in the country's push west.

Mission Accomplished

Lewis and Clark returned successfully. The president had hoped they would discover a river that would take them straight to the Pacific Ocean. Though Lewis and Clark did not find a single river, they did have a path west. It used a mix of rivers and trails.

> Clark made detailed maps of the areas he explored. He published them in 1810 and 1814. They were thought of as the best maps of the west until the 1840s.

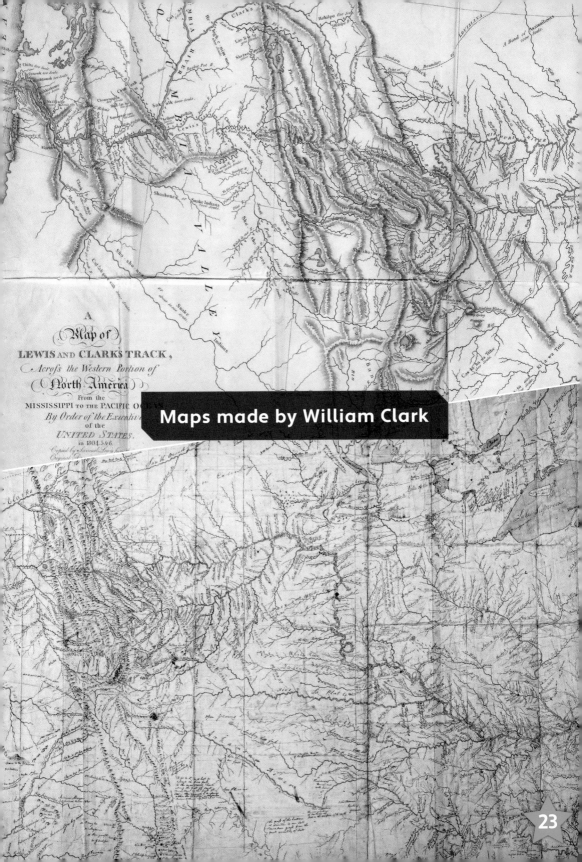
Maps made by William Clark

Members of the expedition also took detailed notes about the things they saw. They brought back journals about the land, plants, and animals. They also learned more about the people living in the area. Their journals would help future explorers headed west.

> Lewis discovered many plants and animals that were new to him. His notes listed 178 kinds of plants. He also wrote about 122 **species** of animals. These included grizzly bears and prairie dogs.

A prairie dog

Just the Beginning

The Lewis and Clark Expedition helped the United States learn more about the west. Thanks to Native guides, the Corps was able to learn about the land, plants, and animals. They learned about the people, too. The whole thing made it possible for Americans to expand west.

> The United States government wanted to control all of the land west of the Louisiana Territory. The Lewis and Clark Expedition began this push.

A Journey of Discovery

Lewis and Clark led an expedition to discover new land. Where did they visit on their journey?

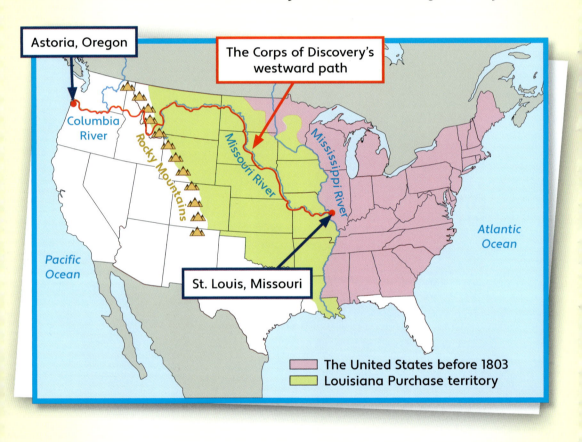

SilverTips for SUCCESS

★ SilverTips for REVIEW

Review what you've learned. Use the text to help you.

Define key terms

expedition
Louisiana Purchase
settlers
territory
The Corps of Discovery

Check for understanding

How did the Louisiana Purchase change the United States?

What were the goals of the Lewis and Clark Expedition?

What role did Native American peoples play in the expedition?

Think deeper

Why was the Lewis and Clark Expedition an important event in the history of the United States?

★ SilverTips on TEST-TAKING

- **Make a study plan.** Ask your teacher what the test is going to cover. Then, set aside time to study a little bit every day.

- **Read all the questions carefully.** Be sure you know what is being asked.

- **Skip any questions** you don't know how to answer right away. Mark them and come back later if you have time.

Glossary

blacksmiths workers who shape metal by heating it and then hammering it

border the line where one place ends and another begins

expedition a long trip taken for a specific reason, such as exploring

mission an important job or task

secretary a person who handles records, letters, and other things for another person

settlers people who live and make a home in a new place

species groups that plants and animals are divided into, according to similar characteristics

territory an area of land controlled by a country

Read More

Chandler, Matt. *The Lewis and Clark Expedition: Separating Fact from Fiction (Fact vs. Fiction in U.S. History).* North Mankato, MN: Capstone Press, 2023.

Harris, Beatrice. *The Lewis and Clark Expedition (A Look at U.S. History).* New York: Gareth Stevens Publishing, 2022.

Lawrence, Blythe. *The Lewis and Clark Expedition (Building Our Nation).* New York: AV2 by Weigl, 2020.

Learn More Online

1. Go to **www.factsurfer.com** or scan the QR code below.
2. Enter "**Lewis and Clark**" into the search box.
3. Click on the cover of this book to see a list of websites.

Index

animals 10, 24, 26
Clark, William 12–14, 20, 22–23, 26, 28
Columbia River 18, 28
Corps of Discovery 12, 14, 16–18, 20, 26, 28
fur trade 10
Lewis, Meriwether 12–14, 20, 22, 24, 26, 28
Louisiana Purchase 6, 8
maps 4, 10, 22–23
Missouri River 14, 18, 28
Pacific Ocean 18, 20, 22, 28
plants 10, 24, 26
President Jefferson, Thomas 8, 10, 12
Rocky Mountains 18, 28
Sacagawea 16–17
settlers 7–8
St. Louis, Missouri 14, 20–21, 28
territory 6–8, 10, 12, 26, 28

About the Author

Daniel R. Faust is a freelance writer of fiction and nonfiction. He lives in Brooklyn, NY.